MW01294553

THE WITCHES' RUNES

A TRADITIONAL DIVINATION SYSTEM

DANA CORBY

THE RANTIN' RAVEN
REVISED EDITION 2018

To Darrell, without whose loving enthusiasm and willingness to buy me computer stuff 25 years ago I could never have done this.

To Wayland Duir, May Farrington, Jay Hedtke, D.B. Myrrha, and many other friends IRL and on Facebook for helping me learn how to turn words into a book in the 21st Century, technological assistance, and holding my hand while I did it.

And to PMH Atwater: Goddess bless, sister Rune-mistress.

Third Printing, 2018 ISBN 9781729220023
The Rantin' Raven
Email: danacorby@centurytel.net

Layout, Design and Rune Images (cover and interior) by Dana Corby

Frontispiece: The Rune Reader © J. Cumming, 1998, used with permission and modified by Dana Corby
All other art public domain.

THE RUNESTONE READER
J. CUMMING, 1993

CONTENTS

INTRODUCTION

Of all the many methods of divination in the world, one of the most ancient and fascinating is the Runestones. As one of the few which belong wholly to the Western magical heritage, owing nothing to the East either for technique or underlying philosophy, the Runestones are – or should be – the one divination system that Witches can claim as our own. It is also, with even a little dedication, one of the easiest systems to learn, often giving spectacular results.

Runestones belong to that class of divination called sortilege. This class or "meta-system" of divination also includes Tarot, I Ching, and geomancy, and is the origin of such customs as drawing for the short straw (lots, which is in turn the origin of the "lottery") and flipping a coin. In Medieval times, the drawing of lots was so respected as a method for divining God's will that it was sometimes actually used in the courts to determine which of several suspects was guilty of a crime.

With the rise of secularism, such practices vanished from public life. Thanks in great part, though, to the romanticizing of Classical and Eastern cultures in the Eighteenth and Nineteenth Centuries, Tarot and the I Ching remained popular if not taken seriously. Astrology, because it was an intellectual, upper-class, and primarily male pursuit, never went away. And of course, every child knows about flipping a coin.

But the Runestones, like the Witches who secretly passed them down through the generations, disappeared from view until the repeal of the last Witchcraft Act in 1951 made it safe for British Witches to step out of the broom closet. Several systems have been published since then, but not until now has their historic relationship to the Craft of the Shapers been so firmly established.

Come, rediscover this ancestral Art…

WHAT ARE RUNES?

The word "Rune" originally meant only those symbols which make up any of the many forms of Futhark, also called runic. This system of esoteric writing and magic developed in Northern Europe, in what are now called Scandinavia and Germany, probably evolving gradually out of prehistoric petroglyphs. But because nobody else could read these Runes and because these "Northmen" had a reputation for being fearsome sorcerers, over millennia "rune" came to mean any writing used primarily for magical purposes.

The Runes, like Hebrew and other ancient writing systems, had a symbolic meaning in addition to their phonetic value, which made the mere writing of them a magical act. Each symbol also had an ideographic meaning such as cow, sheep, measure of grain, bow, etc.

Although we might like to think that writing, including runic, was invented by priests and magi to preserve the Mysteries, it was more likely developed by temple accountants to tally offerings (tithes, really) of commodities: In most of the ancient Near East, Egypt and Minoan Crete, writing was paired with counting to record stores and bills of lading for many centuries before it was ever turned to any other purpose. In Minoan Crete it appears that it was never used for anything but accounting.

The myths tell us the Runes were received by the Aesir (i.e. Norse) father-god Odin as he hung nine days and nights on the World Tree, Yggdrasil. Variants of the myth state that he either was given them by the Giant Mimir as the prize for having endured the test, or he stole them and was hung on the Tree in retribution. But there are too many points of commonality with other, older myths for this to have been the original tale.

The very name Odin, for instance, is just a diminutive for that of a far more ancient God, Od. As God of death and the underworld, part of an incredibly ancient pantheon known as the Vanir (Children of Vana,) Od, like most chthonic Gods, was lord of the underground realm whence came, before the Indo-European invasion, all wisdom. Od, not Odin, is the probable source of the Runes.

The World Tree on which Odin hung is another extremely ancient archetype, the origins of which are almost certainly in the Middle East. Variants appear in Mesopotamia, Egypt, and all over the prehistoric and Bronze Age Mediterranean. Depending on the locale, it was portrayed as a date palm, a fig tree, a grape vine, or, as shown here, a pomegranate bush. Never an apple tree, though, a thousand years of Christian art notwithstanding. A World Tree or Tree of Life is a symbol of farmers and orchardists, people who had to some degree tamed Nature.

Aesir cosmology, on the other hand, saw the forces of nature as inimical to mankind – giants and trolls and ettins – with which humanity was in perpetual war. It seems highly unlikely that they would have conceived of the entire cosmos as arranged in the branches of a great tree. It does seem likely, though, that they received this imagery not directly from Mesopotamia but from an intermediary culture, such as the Vanir-worshippers from whom they borrowed much else including several of their most important Deities.

Finally, and most tellingly, the Aesir-worshippers were a warrior culture, originally nomadic. Such cultures, while usually fine craftsmen, rarely feel much need to leave information behind them.

Writing is a static art; it is also a bulky one, requiring an enormous investment in safe storage. But the bardic or more properly skaldic arts of exact remembering and recital were as compact and portable as the inside of one's skull. It is interesting that when the Aesir-folk did adopt the Runes, they invented ways in which the symbols could be combined or "bound" so that a whole word could occupy the space of a single letter.

The Vanir-folk, on the other hand, were settled people of villages and farms. As later chroniclers attest, they had religious communities that we would recognize as temples, complete with dedicated structures. They had herds, and thus pasture-lands, and their myths indicate a knowledge both of grain-farming and orchardry. These people had a need to keep records, as well as to work magic, and it is with the Vanir that I personally place the origin of the Futhark.

But the word "rune," with its variants in most European languages, does not mean just the Futhark. It refers to concepts of mystery, secrets, and magic. Thus it eventually came to mean any kind of magical or occult symbol, not just those from the Futhark. A number of Medieval and

Renaissance magical alphabets such as Theban and Passing the River – mere transliteration codes for Hebrew and Latin – are also sometimes called Runes, as were Gypsy marks, Ogham, and even the Enochian script of Dr. John Dee, court astrologer to Elizabeth I.

Because of the perceived power of runic magic, any magical writings and recitations, such as spells or cantrips, also came to be called Runes, even when written in plain English. A modern example is Doreen Valiente's famous spell-poem which begins "Darksome night and shining moon...," and is titled *The Witch's Rune*.

THE RUNESTONES

Waves of settlement by Northern peoples, notably the Saxons and Angles, brought the Futhark to Britain. And in Britain the history of the Runes took a radical turn.

On the Continent, the term *Runestones* referred to what we would call monuments: standing stones carved with runes, pictographs, and other symbols. Such Runestones served as funerary monuments, boundary-markers, battle memorials, and many other magical, commemorative and practical purposes.

But in Britain, the same word came to mean a collection of pebbles, each marked with a different rune or symbol, which were used for divination. This appears to have been a particularly British art, since none of the major works on Continental rune-magic refer to it.

Long after runic was supplanted in Britain by the Latin alphabet, the Runestones continued to be used for divination, although other symbols began to be included among the original Runes. Several different Runestone systems (no doubt once many) have been preserved, along with many other ancient crafts and customs, by the people we now know as Witches: the inheritors of the native magic tradition of the British Isles.

Several British sources mention the Runestones as traditional to Witches: Arnold & Patricia Crowther, Janet & Stewart Farrar, and Rhiannon Ryall, to name a few. Some of the material suggests that the use of Runestones by Witches is far older and more traditional than the Tarot or any divination system except perhaps scrying.

The first popularizer of Runestone divination in the U. S., Ralph Blum, claimed to possess the only authentic system, on the basis of having received it from an elderly British hereditary Witch. While that does not necessarily validate Blum's claim to exclusivity, it does, along with the actual Witch authors noted, support a connection between the Runestones and Witches.

The version in the Crowthers' "Lid Off the Cauldron" and that in Ryall's "West Country Wicca," while both undeniably Runestones, are quite distinct in both markings and technique from Blum's and from each other. The system I was taught is different from all of them. Yet there are enough similarities between these various systems that I feel confident in ascribing a common origin in the British Isles.

Even so, no non-Germanic system in use today is made entirely of Runes from any form of the Futhark; the Crowther version, for instance, is comprised entirely of non-Futhark symbols. The system in this book is made up of just over half Futhark, with the rest being runic-looking glyphs and, for "money," the alchemical sign for the sun and gold.

It seems clear that variations in the Runestones occurred as some symbols ceased to have any meaning for people and others, such as that alchemical sun sign or the leafy branch "luck" sign in the Crowthers' system, took on significance. Like the beers and cheeses for which the British Isles are also famous, these variations were probably originally specific to a particular region, or even to one little village.

Today there are two schools of thought surrounding the use of old artifacts, such as the Runes, that once belonged to a particular culture: reconstructionism and eclecticism. The reconstructionists hold that such things ought to be preserved exactly as they were, and if used at all, used only as their creators did. The eclectics hold that our ancestors freely borrowed whatever worked from each other's cultures and that we are equally free to do so.

This is essentially a folk art, and like all such arts it is subject to what they call the "folk process:" the gradual changing of things being passed on due to variables ranging from creative genius to faulty memory. So those divination systems of modern design which look like and work like Runestones are certainly entitled to call themselves that. They do seem to work as well as the ones with a history, if not to possess the glamour of ancientness.

Credit for the Runestones as we know them must go to the generations of British Witches who hid them and continued to teach them for the last fifteen hundred years.

THEORY

Like all forms of sortilege, the Runestones function by the action of the unconscious mind communicating with the conscious.

The unconscious, it is believed by occultists and mystics and definitely by Witches, is at all times in contact with the Infinite, and thus with infinite information. By an act of will, this unconscious connection can be brought to focus on a question. The laws of chance are thus altered; the random fall of the stones or sticks, the shuffle of the cards, is bent out of true random, and they fall in meaningful patterns that can be interpreted by the conscious mind.

Modern psychology is discovering that the primary function of the conscious mind may not after all be the gathering and classifying of information, as our Western, materially-based culture has long assumed, but the filtering out of most of the input we constantly receive from the unconscious. People in whom this filter does not function often wind up in mental institutions. People who learn to turn it off and on at will often become mystics, seers, magicians, and (it would seem) science fiction or fantasy writers.

The phenomenon of subconscious or unconscious access to information was documented by the famed psychologist C. G. Jung, who called it synchronicity. Another name might be "coincidence control," since persons with good awareness of this constant flow of data often seem preternaturally lucky.

In sortilege, the diviner manipulates objects, giving the conscious mind something to play with and to make patterns with: it distracts it, allowing information to come through from the unconscious in forms the diviner can understand; it is often interpreted as a message or forms a story. Sometimes it even seems as if someone (Someone?) is speaking these messages.

The other major form of divination, scrying, is also performed by the action of the unconscious, but the connection is made in an entirely

11

different way. Scrying, the use of a crystal, a dark mirror, or some other focus to "see" what otherwise could not be seen, works by stilling the conscious mind and allowing direct imagery to come through from that unconscious connection with infinity.

Which of the two techniques will work for a particular person is a matter mostly of whether they tend to be introverted or extroverted, to seek meaning within themselves or in the external world.

Interpreting the Runestones is a function of *patterning*, that most basic activity of the sentient mind. All purposeful activity is the result of making or seeking patterns, whether it is the map-dance and geometric architecture of the honeybee or the formal abstractions of the human mathematician. In the cast of the Runestones we see patterns – lines, triangles, squares, pentagons, and more – that connect the simple ideograms of each rune into something like sentences, and those sentences into stories.

The point must be made that there is nothing supernatural about divination, although it is certainly magical. Like patterning, the ability to do magic is inherent in all human beings. It is only the acculturation of modern, materialist society which convinces people that such things are not real and anyone who thinks they can do magic is crazy or possessed. But you can. To learn more about freeing ourselves from this repressive mind-set, I recommend the blog post "Re-Enchanting the World" by Kingsley Dennis.

All you need to reclaim these natural abilities is to focus the will and learn a few basic skills, and to practice. There will be differences in talent, of course just as in everything. After all, every able-bodied human can run, but few of us make it to the Olympics. It's worth doing for its own sake, just the same.

DIVINATION ETHICS

It is perhaps most important, and most difficult, to free yourself from what the 19th century occultist Aleister Crowley called "lust of result." Learn to care only for the truth, not for having your own opinions validated or for being able to tell your "client" (for want of a better word) what they want to hear. This is the difference between true divination and parlor games – or bunco.

If you are serious about developing your skill with the Runestones, and about your Craft in general, it will be important to you to give accurate readings. The best way to keep track is to keep a journal of all your readings. Record both your own perceptions and those of whomever you read for.

After six months to a year, you may feel that you can dispense with the  journal. If you make divination the keystone of your Craft work, however, or make part of your living by it, you should probably continue recording results. At any rate, divination done as part of Coven or private Circle work should always be included in your usual notes.

If you charge for readings, there is a very good reason, besides your own sense of honor, to always give the best reading you can: to avoid being charged with fraud.

When I was first taught, forty-plus years ago, Craft law did not permit initiated Witches to take money for the use of their arts. Period. Times have changed, thank the Gods, and it is now recognized as ethical to profit from the practice of one's skills, though we of course still do not charge for religious teaching or coven membership. But the authorities may have other ideas.

There are some very peculiar laws around regarding "fortune-telling." Some places still have what used to be called gypsy laws on the books, defining certain (or all) forms of divination as fortune-telling and all fortune-telling as fraud. A few places even make it a crime to teach divination or to sell supplies, as if they were drugs or pornography.

As an example of how silly this can get, consider the small towns of Montclair and Clairmont, next to each other in the foothills east of Los Angeles. Both had gypsy laws; they may still. In one, astrology was legal but you couldn't read or sell Tarot cards; in the other, Tarot was legal but not the practice or even teaching of astrology!

The L.A. County ordinances merely forbade charging for divination, though you could accept donations as long as you didn't even *hint* at an appropriate amount. This is the law under which the prominent feminist Witch Z. Budapest, in a nationally notorious case, was prosecuted many years ago. She charged an undercover vice officer five dollars for a Tarot reading that the officer candidly admitted in court was absolutely accurate and well worth the five dollars.

It is easy and simple to call your local police department and ask what the ordinances are, and it is not necessary to identify yourself. You will get your information, avoid trouble, and completely astound the officer you talk to: they are not used to having people ask before they break the law.

Be mindful also
of the Law of Threefold Return:
What you put forth returns thrice-fold.

If you fake it, or give garbage readings,
you will soon be unable to give any other kind.

There are all sorts of rational sounding explanations of
why this happens, but Witches believe that the Gods
give us these abilities so that we may guide our lives in
accordance with Their will, in harmony with the Life of
the Universe. When you prostitute this great gift, it is
withdrawn.

It's that simple.

14

THIS SYSTEM

This Runestone system came to me in 1972 as part of my original training in the Craft. I was told by my teacher, Lady Sara, that they were traditional. While research has enabled me to place their probable origin in Britain, I cannot trace them to any individual before Lady Sara, an American. What follows, then, is a written record of a tradition previously passed on only by oral transmission, plus the results of my more than forty years' experience and experimentation with divining by the Runestones.

Traditionally, this set consists of fourteen Runestones and two unmarked stones of a different color and shape. These represent the querent, the person for whom you are reading: a round one for a female querent and a longish one for a male. This is more evidence for a deep connection between Runestones and British Witchcraft, since almost all the old Craft traditions emphasize gender polarity in their magical practices.

But in these times our concepts of gender and identity are changing rapidly, and the traditional querents may not always be appropriate. If you or your client prefer not to be identified as male or female, I suggest you add a gender-neutral querent stone to your set. I guarantee that like my "Group" querent, it will work just fine.

Not long after I started reading for a coven I was in, I discovered that whichever Querent I used tended to give a reading for the corresponding coven leader, not for the coven as a group. So one evening I walked out into their back yard, picked up a rock about the right size, walked back in and announced "This one means 'Group.' " It worked like it had always been part of the set.

The concepts expressed by the individual Runestones are so simple as to seem skeletal. There is none of the philosophical overlay (or depths, if you prefer,) of the Tarot or I Ching. This lack of baggage is one of the things I like best about them. The stone marked with the rune meaning "man," for instance, does not also carry somebody else's concept of what it means to be male. It merely represents a man who has or will have

15

some bearing on the question. This simplicity gives great flexibility in interpreting a reading. It also has its limitations, which we address below.

If you research runic, you will find that the Runes do indeed have elaborate esoteric meanings. But as symbols within a divination system, they are outside that stream of runic lore, and need mean no more than the attributions given them here. Some of the other symbols also have meanings within their original systems, but here they don't.

The one disadvantage to such simplicity, of course, is that sometimes a question will be put for which the Runes are not quite adequate. In these cases, you can temporarily assign a special meaning to the stone or stones which come closest to expressing the required concepts. If you must rename more than two or at the most three stones, it would probably be best to use a more elaborate divination system for the question.

To avoid any possibility of contaminating the reading, rename the stones before beginning the reading but after being told the question – you have to know what to name it. A particular person's name might be given to the man or woman stone, for example, or a specific issue to the disordered thoughts rune. Always unname the stones afterward, or you can get some very odd readings from then on.

FORMULA OF NAMING & UNNAMING

Touch your right (dominant hand) forefinger to the rune you wish to rename.

- Recite the formula of naming:
  "Runestone called (usual name,) for this divination I name you
  _____"

- Trace the *invoking* pentagram three times above the stone.

INVOKING   BANISHING

16

- When the reading is over, again touch the named stone, saying: "The reading is ended, and it is time to resume your true name. I remove from you the name of _____" (trace the *banishing* pentagram three times above the stone) "... and restore to you, your true name of (usual name.)"

- Again trace the *invoking* pentagram above the stone. Return it to the rest of the set.

This system has grown considerably more sophisticated in the more than forty years I have practiced it. Like the original evolution from petroglyph to pictogram to ideograph to rune, these methods have evolved through oral teaching, experimentation and just plain mutation. In fact, a radical variant on this system, that of feminist writer P.M.H. Atwater, is listed in the Bibliography.

Once you have mastered the methods given here, I hope you will add your own refinements, interpret the symbols in ways that give them meaning for you, and develop a magical relationship with them.

Above all, don't feel that because anything about them is "in the book" it's The Truth and unchangeable. Onewayism has no place in the Craft, or in any of its Arts.

CASTING & READING

GENERAL ADVICE:

- If you usually consecrate your magical tools, you will probably want to do so with your Runestones. I was originally taught never to let anyone else touch my tools, including my Runestones, and I do keep one set that no one handles but myself. But since it is standard procedure in other divination systems for the client to handle the cards or sticks or whatever, and nothing untoward happens, I tried allowing my clients to handle my unconsecrated set. Frankly, I have found no difference in the results. Decide for yourself how you feel about people touching your Runestones.

- Don't ever "force" a reading. If the pattern just makes no sense, give up and try again another time. Similarly, don't try to give too many readings one after the other: as you tire, your accuracy drops off. This can undermine your confidence. Worse, it could tempt you to fudge a reading. If on the other hand an answer seems to leap out at you immediately, it is probably correct. Go with it.

- If you routinely read for a group such as a family or coven, you may find it very helpful to acquire the "Group" Querent stone described in Chapter 5. While not exactly traditional, it works well, as would a gender-neutral Querent should you decide to use one.

- Any time one stone drops out of your hand while you are handling them before the reading, it has special meaning. Some previously ignored facet of the question is yelling "Look at me!" If the DEATH stone does so, this is a sign to abort the reading.

By the way – the DEATH stone does not automatically mean someone is going to die! I have only once ever gotten a reading in which the DEATH-rune actually meant death: a coworker's goldfish all died while she was on vacation.

PREPARATION

Clarity and detachment are crucial to a successful Runestone reading. Formulate the question in your mind, or if you are reading for another, help them to articulate it as clearly as possible. Know what you want to know, and why: many times, what seems a totally irrelevant reading will actually be addressing what is really on your mind. As in all magic, fuzzy intentions get fuzzy results.

Before beginning a Runestone reading, spend a while clearing your mind, and if you know the technique, centering. This may be as elaborate as a full Circle Casting or as simple as a few deep breaths, as circumstances or your inclinations dictate, but here is a simple centering ritual:

CENTERING RITUAL

- Close your eyes. Take a deep breath and let it out slowly. Again. And again.

- As you continue breathing, understand your energies, your thoughts, your emotions, as scattered sparks of your true Self, flying off in all directions.

- Now imagine sending out a shining net of light and warmth and Self, big enough and fine enough to encompass them all.

- Draw the net in, gently. It gets smaller and brighter as you pull it toward you. All the way in, to the very Center of your being. Some people feel their Center in their solar plexus, the energy center just below the breastbone. Some experience it behind their navel. Wherever yours resides, tuck that energy-filled net in there. Give it a moment to settle in and be calm.

- Empty the Runestone pouch into your hands, returning any stone you will not be using to the pouch. Gently pour the stones from hand to hand for a while as you concentrate on the question and ask for spiritual aid. Feel the trance-like calm this creates. Feel the stones taking up your body heat, and yourself giving up your tensions. Feel yourself becoming attuned to the stones, the question, the moment.

Now you are ready.

CASTING

The expression for using the Runestones is to "cast" them, and that is exactly how it is done, with a gentle toss. Remember to use the correct querent stone even when reading for yourself. Gather the fourteen marked stones and the appropriate querent into your hands, center (see above,) and when you feel the moment is right, cast them onto a flat surface and begin to study the patterns they form. Because this system is so flexible, there are several different methods for both casting and interpreting the Runestones; all of them depend upon the patterning and intuitional skills of the reader.

METHODS OF READING

Over the years, a number of different methods for reading a Runestone cast have evolved for me, as different circumstances required a different approach to the problem. Become familiar to all of them, as they make this a much more flexible and thus more effective divinatory tool. You will no doubt find that one method becomes your "old standby" favorite, but you must be able to adapt to the needs of those you read for. The first listing, the Basic Reading, is the way I was originally taught to read the stones. All the rest are the result of experience and/or inspiration.

1: BASIC READING

This reading seems to work best for events over a time-span of not more than a month or two. Experiment and see for yourself.

- Cast the Runes. Turn all stones so their Runes show, being careful not to move them otherwise.
- Start reading at the querent stone and spiral out in all directions. Those stones closest to the querent are either closer in time or more important to the question, becoming more remote as they move away. If one or two stones come to rest quite a distance from the rest and do not seem to be part of the overall pattern, they probably have no bearing on the question.
- Take into account the ways in which the stones are grouped and interpret them in terms of these relationships as much as their

relationship to the querent. Note the way tight clusters or geometric figures make the stones seem to support or oppose each other, how a row of stones leading from the perimeter towards the querent (or vice versa) may lend a sense of inevitability or that events are moving quickly.

- Pay attention to whether the overall pattern clusters near the querent or is more open, whether the querent (and thus your client) seems to be in the midst of things or somewhat detached. Generally speaking, if the querent stone rests at the near edge of the casting pattern it means that the events are in the future; at the far edge, we're seeing the past.

2: "QUICK AND DIRTY" READING

Cast the Runes as usual. Read only those stones which lie face up, for a look at the major factors and influences on the question. Interpret them just as in the Basic Reading. Some Runestone readers always use this method, feeling (not without merit) that not every rune-concept is always relevant. In my own practice, though, I've found that the irrelevant Runes tend to opt out of the pattern.

3: "LAYERED" READING

For greater detail about the varying degrees of importance of the different Runes, make a sketch of the reading layout before beginning to read it, and before turning up any stones which lie face down. Treat those stones which are face up as primary influences on the question, and deal with them first.

Now turn the remaining stones face up and mark these Runes in on your sketch, perhaps in a different color ink to make it easier to remember which is which. These stones represent either secondary, less important, influences, or they can represent past-life issues. It is up to you and your client to determine which, perhaps by deciding ahead of time that you would like to explore past life influences on a present problem. It will probably fall to the client rather than the reader to determine the relative importance of past-life and present-life influences.

4: CASTING ON A FIELD

Casting the stones onto a design or "field" can add another kind of detail to a reading. Using a large sheet of paper, create one of the following:

- Divide the area in half, designating one side "yes," the other, "no." The pros and cons of a difficult decision can be examined in detail and at leisure.

- Divide the field into thirds to represent any one of the many triads, such as past, present, and future; Maiden, Mother and Crone; body, mind, and spirit. There are many.

- If you have a basic knowledge of astrology, casting the Runestones onto a 12-house field can be very illuminating. For the more advanced practitioner, a large copy of your (or your client's) natal horoscope can form the basis for a Runestone "progression." Place the querent stone on the existing Sun position, and cast the rest of the stones by either the basic or layered method.

Other fields could include the Tree of Life, the Druidic Circles of Existence, or any meaningful mandala. Anything which catches your imagination can be meaningful and thus add meaning to your readings. If you find that you get enjoyment and good results from using a particular field, make a permanent one of fabric, consecrate it, and consider it part of the set.

5: GROUP READING

Every group takes on a kind of "group soul," with a life-force of its own and a unique identity on the other planes. This group identity is what a group reading reads..

There are two different techniques for doing a group reading. I find the second of the two much more fun and usually far more accurate, though there are times when only the first will do.

It is especially important, when reading for a group, to make sure that all participants agree about the question to be asked and the exact wording of the question.

A: SINGLE CASTER

- Cast as usual, using the "group" querent stone. Be sure to name it (remember to unname it afterwards.) This method can be used to do an absent reading for a group as you can for an individual.

- In a group reading those stones which represent people will indicate non-members; the members are submerged in the group identity represented by the querent stone.

B: GROUP CASTING

- Have all participants stand in a circle.

- Place all the stones in a container except the querent, which is placed on the floor in the middle of the circle.

- Walk around the circle allowing each participant to take a stone, without looking, from the container.
  If there are more stones than people, you can either keep circulating until all stones have been taken or you can consider that left-over stones have no bearing on the question.
  If there are more people than stones, have those who did not get a stone move around the circle so that they are standing between people who do; they place a hand on the shoulder on each side of them to form a link.

- Now each person looks at their stone(s.) Starting with the first person to draw a stone from the bowl, each person tosses their stone as close as possible to the querent.

- When all the stones have been thrown, read the pattern; reading all the stones as in the Basic Reading.

- Now ask each person in turn to talk about the stone they drew and how it relates both to the question at hand and their own situation. It is always relevant and often uncanny.

Most readers like to thank their Runestones before returning them to their pouch or box. You may like to ritually cleanse them from time to time, as well. Burying them in salt overnight is a time-honored method, as is leaving them outside under the rays of the full moon.

THE RUNES & THEIR MEANINGS

The Rune symbols are presented here in the order in which I received them. The first four seem to represent a logical progression, but after that the order appears random.

MAN

A male other than the Querent. The Futhark rune Elhaz; Anglo-Saxon Eolh. It may originally have been a pictogram representing antlers, as the literal meaning is "elk."

WOMAN

A female other than the querent. One of the non-Futhark symbols, this is nonetheless ancient, and may represent a broom, a skirt wearer, or (reversed) the female pubis.

LOVE

The first two Runes, superimposed, form the symbol for LOVE. Usually taken to mean romantic love but depending on its position in the reading and the nature of the question can mean familial, spiritual, and other kinds of love.

FAMILY

The LOVE rune, plus "children." This can mean blood relations or family-by-affiliation such as spouse (and in-laws,) life-mate, coven or commune. To someone very emotionally attached to their work, this rune could even represent their employees or coworkers.

THE HOME

The querent's dwelling place, their family home or property; can represent the covenstead in group readings, and often stands for one's place of business. This non-Futhark rune depicts the most ancient magical definition of a dwelling: a roof and a threshold.

GIFTS

Futhark Gebo, Anglo-Saxon Gyfu, and not all that much changed after all these centuries. Stands for unexpected windfalls, legacies, presents, promotions – things of value acquired outside the usual sorts of compensation. Depending on context can also mean charity; if conjunct with POISON, nasty strings are attached.

MONEY

The astrological sign for the sun, which rules gold, which means money. All monetary or material concerns; used also for business questions. Appearing with the GIFTS or POSSESSIONS rune, it implies they have greater value than might be expected. As with GIFTS, the presence of POISON with MONEY indicates negative under-currents or consequences.

POSSESSIONS

Futhark Othala, Anglo-Saxon Öthel, both meaning property in the sense of real estate. Modern usage also includes valuable personal property. In the Old Norse this rune is named Odhal; it implies a person's nature or inborn qualities. Thus, this rune means "what you own and what you are" and is often pivotal in interpreting a reading.

POISON

Another rune from an unknown source. It represents negativity feeding into the situation from the outside, deliberate or even unconscious poisoning of the energy. Includes gossip, slander, office politics, meddling, back-stabbing and hidden agendas of all kinds. To remember it easily, think of it as the Dirty Double Cross.

DISORDERED THOUGHTS

Of unknown origin, but a fine ideograph for concepts related to confusion, quibbling, internal negativity (as opposed to the external POISON,) irrationality, stress, even mental illness and madness. Most often, it means that the querent is indecisive or in denial, but it can indicate something serious.

WAR

This non-Futhark rune represents any overt conflict, quarrel, ongoing disagreement, or feud. It rarely means actual military action; but it certainly can. The symbol appears to be created with two Man Runes which simultaneously oppose and support each other, thus expressing the warrior ideal.

DEATH

Futhark Eihwaz, Anglo-Saxon Eoh, which both mean "yew." The yew has been an emblem of death from time immemorial for its poisonous berries and its tough wood, so perfect for making bows. Because it is an evergreen, it also stands for rebirth after death. This stone indicates cessation, end of a matter, radical transformation or abrupt change of situation. Often shows that a particular situation is about to end, or will be of short duration.

COMFORT

Anglo-Saxon Wynn, Futhark Wunjo: pleasure, joy, delight. This rune is one of the more difficult to interpret, as it can mean things as diverse as enjoyment of life, emotional security, being well fed and warm, or one's ability to accept – be comfortable with – new or alien ideas. Depending on placement, can indicate a need to reassess one's root assumptions

FIRE

Kenaz in the Futhark, Cen (pronounced "keen") in Anglo-Saxon; it means torch. This rune is an intensifier, adding the traditional meanings of fire to those stones around it. It heats things up, adds passion, emphasis, speed, enthusiasm, or physicality. When together with the LOVE stone, read as "lust."

Until you have all the Rune meanings memorized, you may wish to keep a list of the Runes and their names with your set.

About 20 years ago I drew mine in Sharpie on a piece of white cotton cloth so I could fold it small without creasing it to death, and I still carry it. Only now I hand it to the client. This greatly helps their ability to follow and understand the reading, and gives them a tactile way to relate to it.

SAMPLE READINGS

The ideal way to learn the art of reading the Runestones is to sit in while an experienced reader does readings and explains aloud how they arrive at their interpretations. The information is absorbed holistically, with instruction, observation, and interaction taking place simultaneously. Depending on the innate ability of the student and the degree of intuitional communication with the teacher, this can take anything from an hour to months.

In a written form, the teaching must be separated into theory, which we've already covered, and specific examples, which we will explore in this chapter. It is not as well-rounded a method as direct teaching, but it has advantages: the student can choose the pace and order of the lessons, the times of study and practice, so it's far less stressful: a book never makes you feel like an idiot if you make mistakes. The advantage to the teacher is that things only have to be explained once. This, too, is far less stressful!

These examples are not concrete illustrations of how to read this-or-that layout. It cannot be over-emphasized that there are no "layouts" with the Runestones, only patterns. All the Runestones are, in the end, is a handle for your mind to grasp what your intuition knows. Please remember that a particular grouping of stones may mean one thing in these examples and something entirely different given other circumstances and participants.

For ease in interpreting, these examples assume Basic Reading style. Imagine them spread out on a table in front of you, with the bottom of the picture as the near table-edge.

FIRST READING

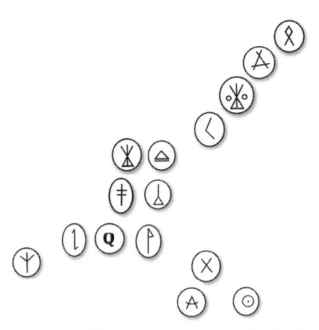

Single woman, around 30 years old, accountant. She has been having trouble with her boyfriend and would like to know whether her suspicions about him are correct.

The first thing we notice here is that the MAN rune, which we would assume means the boyfriend, is way off by itself, as if it had nothing to do with the question. This is rather odd, and should be brought to the Querent's attention so that it can be explored. Next we notice that the Querent stone itself is bracketed by DEATH and COMFORT. I feel strongly that this indicates a major and probably abrupt transition, a change in comfortable habits or challenge to long-held assumptions. The Querent seems caught or balanced between entropy and change, never a comfortable position.

Above the Querent stone (farther away from the reader – that's you) and about the same distance as the last two, we have WOMAN; this stone is conjunct to POISON, part of a grouping which also includes LOVE and THE HOME. Four different patterns occur here, each with its own significance.

All four stones taken together may indicate a woman (not the Querent, remember) poisoning – bringing negative energy to – the loving home environment of the Querent and her boyfriend. The energy here seems to be moving away from the Querent; I get an impression of old business not properly concluded.

The triad of LOVE, the HOME, and POISON seems significant but is hard to pin down. A need for elbow room, perhaps? There may be a need for a good psychic cleansing of the living space and purification of the couple.

The LOVE, POISON, WOMAN group curves slightly to "sideswipe" the Querent and move the attention back into the COMFORT stone. This reinforces the idea that the Querent and her current situation are about to be shaken up and that the person moving the energy is not the boyfriend but the unknown woman. On being asked, the Querent says that the boyfriend has a mother, a sister, and two ex-wives, any one of whom might have reasons to interfere in her relationship with him, some through malice and some through real concern for the Querent.

From here we drop back into the pattern in the lower right corner. This triad of GIFTS, WAR, and MONEY is not uncommon in situations of conflict between family members and lovers when a break-up is imminent, and "ours" starts reverting to "mine" and "yours." The issues over who gave what to whom, and how much it's worth, can get nasty. In this case, though, I think it may not be gifts between the Querent and her boyfriend as much as from the boyfriend to the as-yet unknown woman in the previous grouping. The question pops into my mind: does he have any children? Yes. Ah, child support fight? Yes, she answers.

Moving back again to the plane "above" the Querent, we have a straight line of four stones beginning off to the right of the Querent and marching purposefully into the future: FIRE, FAMILY, DISORDERED THOUGHTS and a little separated, POSSESSIONS. Now FIRE is an adjective stone, adding power and passion to the stones near it; I interpret it in this position as relating primarily to FAMILY but somewhat to COMFORT. The latter seems to indicate a real problem with clinging to what needs to change. This reinforces the ideas in the first part of the reading. As it relates to FAMILY, however, I see strong family ties and loyalties on the one hand and deep ambivalence (disordered thoughts) on the other. The position of POSSESSIONS would indicate a need – perhaps unacknowledged – for the Querent to take stock of her possessions, those things which make her uniquely herself without regard for family or familial-feeling relationships.

Having explored each grouping, the reading is finished with a recap or overview. It is always necessary to put things in a way that is likely to be accepted by the listener, to temper truth with diplomacy. In this case, I did not tell the young lady that she had dependency problems and that her love was a jerk, though I got both those impressions fairly strongly.

I talked about needing to be prepared for major life-changes and for things to not be quite what they seemed. I pointed out that the multiple ladies in this situation made accuracy difficult, since the stones can indicate gender but not number; however, given the child support issue it seemed likely that the "mystery woman" was the mother of the child. I also pointed out that when a woman is owed back child support she has good reason to put out negativity about the father and for his current lady (the Querent) to wonder just how much she could count on him if there were problems... or a child.

I advised that she take stock of her own strengths and good qualities – those things she likes best about herself – and use that knowledge in the coming months. Reminding her of the strong emphasis on change and transition, I advised flexibility and willingness to examine her ideas about the way things are "supposed" to be. And I concluded with my impression that the boyfriend had in all probability not been entirely honest about himself. In particular, I was concerned about his pattern of irresponsibility towards women and a general lack of willingness to take responsibility for his own actions.

SECOND READING

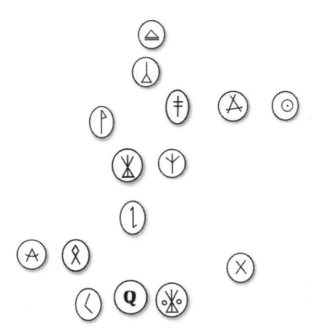

Married woman, about 30 years old, "writer and mom" who works part time in a small shop. Six months pregnant. Feels blocked in her writing, would like to know why.

This is one of those readings that are very easy to answer on the surface but then require some thought. The Querent stone is bracketed by FAMILY and FIRE, telling us that this woman puts most of her energy into her family. It's obvious her writing doesn't progress because she does not give it first priority. No value judgment is attached to that observation; only she can say where her energies are best spent. However, recognizing and acknowledging that she is making the choice herself to do other things than write can help her to make decisions about that choice and then make peace with herself about it.

Farther away, though, things are not so clear-cut. To the left and "up" a bit, we have WAR paired with POSSESSIONS. I wondered aloud if one of the reasons she is not taking the time her writing needs is that someone in the family gets angry or makes it a struggle; POSSESSIONS in this case being personal attributes rather than goods.

Off to the right, at about the same distance, GIFTS stands alone and rather inscrutable. Its proximity to the Querent would seem to mean that it is significant, but its lack of relationship to other stones makes it impossible to interpret.

Straight up from the Querent, feeling central to the reading, is DEATH, the stone of transitions and transformations. When I mentioned this very significant event, she laughed and at that time told me she was pregnant. This being the nature of the transitional event, the next two stones are obvious: MAN and LOVE together signify her husband. He is not well "aspected" (as the astrologers say,) as he is also paired with POISON, the stone of outside negativity coming into a situation. Perhaps he is the source of the WAR vibe earlier on.

Forming a horizontal bar with POISON are DISORDERED THOUGHTS and MONEY. She may feel pressured by her husband to get a "real" job instead of writing, a notoriously financially shaky profession.

I also got a strong intuitive impression that the root of the conflict may well be that she has the ambivalence of many women towards money, and especially towards engaging in the arts or letters for profit. To the left of these three Runes is COMFORT, still on the same plane but feeling detached from the rest. It seems to relate more directly with LOVE and MAN, and to form a pentagon both with those two and with POISON and WOMAN.

The first formation, the triangle, seems to signify that her relationship with her husband may be too comfortable, or that she is making assumptions about it that may not be true. The POISON/WOMAN addition to the equation may mean that there is danger to the relationship from a female. As the WOMAN stone is paired with THE HOME, I wonder if the new child will be a girl, and if her birth might not portend trouble – possibly financial in nature –to the stability of the family or the querent's ambitions.

This reading, in the end, is a lot of "maybe's." The impending birth of a child multiplies the possible paths into the future past any hope of accurate divination. If I were to advise this woman as to the best course of action for the near future, though, I would say that she needs to continue putting her family first, and if she is serious about writing, to learn some effective time-management techniques. I wish her well.

THIRD READING

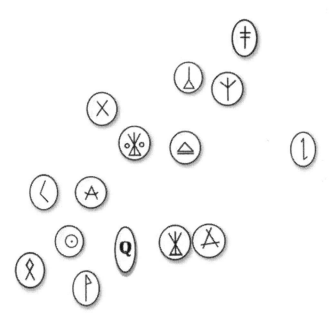

Gay man, 23, full-time English major.

This young man had recently broken up with a somewhat older lover and wanted to know if there was any chance of their reconciliation.

It was hard not to look at the stones in this reading and just say "When hell freezes over, maybe." To the right of the Querent stone is the crux of the problem: LOVE and DISORDERED THOUGHTS not just conjunct but touching. Like many people his age, of whatever orientation, he really doesn't know what he means by the word "love."

To the left of the Querent, we have the cause of the conflict with the ex-lover: bitter fights (WAR and FIRE) over issues of money and lifestyle

(MONEY, POSSESSIONS and COMFORT.)

He confirmed that this had been the case. Straight ahead of the Querent, FAMILY and the HOME are conjunct. I had the impression that he might have been rejected by his family for his orientation, and have developed unrealistic images of what these things mean.

Farther out, and "floating" between HOME/FAMILY and WAR/FIRE, is GIFTS. At first I couldn't interpret it. But something about the way he hesitated to answer questions in this area made me suspect that he might be fulfilling some of his financial needs – and what college student doesn't continually need money? – by prostitution. This in turn seemed somehow connected to the next two stones: Beside the HOME/FAMILY pair we have WOMAN and MAN.

These stones usually refer to specific individuals, but with POISON directly above them, I got the feeling that in this case they referred to unresolved questions of gender identity. This is a difficult issue to talk about to a client: he is likely to get defensive and negate the effectiveness of the reading. In any case, there could be no hope of getting back together with a lover until these questions are answered (and they may have been the reason for the fighting, money issues just acting as camouflage.) So I phrased it as "needing to learn, first, what you really want out of life." Finally, DEATH is way off in right field, unrelated to the rest of the reading. Resolution is not likely to take place any time soon.

My overview of this reading is that, rather than answering this young man's question directly, the forces which work through the Runes give him a comprehensive look at the issues and behaviors which were making it impossible for him to have the love and closeness he so desperately craved. It also dropped some hints, and heavily at that, as to what he needed to change in order to get what he wanted.

Whether he'll ever make those changes, I'll never know. But his energy was fresh and rather sweet, even younger than his youthful chronological age. I think what he needs most is good old *time.*

Hopefully, these three very different readings will give you a better idea how to cast and read The Witches' Runes. Again, I can't emphasize too much that the interpretations are very fluid and that each stone must be read in terms of how it influences, and is influenced by, the stones around it. At the same time, do not be afraid to go with an intuitional reading that leaps out at you even when the stones don't seem to support it: your unconscious is seeing patterns your eyes miss.

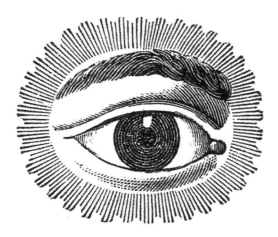

If you still have questions, I enjoy answering them. Please don't hesitate to contact me by email or on Facebook – the information is at both ends of the book.

MAKING YOUR OWN

My first set of The Witches' Runes was made of large, black and white Mexican beach pebbles provided by Lady Sara. We just painted on the Runes, let them dry overnight, and started using them. That worked fine – for a while. But every time I used them a little bit of paint would chip off, and I got tired of constantly repainting them. So I borrowed an electric engraving pen and etched the designs into the surface of the stones. That worked fine for a while, too, but the stones picked up the oils from my hands and soon the etched lines were nearly invisible. So then I washed off the oils and painted over the etched lines. That worked perfectly, and that's how I've made them for the last forty-plus years.

But the Mexican beach pebbles came with their own problem, namely that they're large: a good inch in diameter by up to a half-inch thick. That doesn't sound like much until you recall that you're working with fifteen of them at once! And at the time, before crafts stores like JoAnn's™ and Michael's™ were everywhere, the only place I could find smooth black and white rocks was either a florists' supplier or a garden store, and they were all that big or bigger. What to do?

The answer, for a long time, was not to use rocks at all. I switched to glass. Those glass 'globs,' like flattened marbles, that are available in just about every crafts-shop or dollar-store in the country. At first I stuck with black and white, like the beach pebbles. But one day a prospective client asked if I could do red. Why not? So for about fifteen years I made The Witches' Runes in all colors of the rainbow.

And then I moved to my little piece of paradise, an island in Puget Sound. And walking the beach, I discovered not sand but millions of pebbles, many of them perfect for Runestones. So now I can offer my clients real stones gathered on our beautiful beach. Occasionally, I even make them from tumbled semi-precious stones like crystal or rose quartz.

But you want to know how to make your own.

- If you don't have access to a beach, packages of those smooth black-or-white rocks are now available in much smaller sizes in crafts stores, hobby shops, even dollar stores. And so are the glass globs, if you'd rather go for color.

- Engraving tools start at about $8 US, though I long ago graduated to (and prefer) a Dremel™ with a wider array of tips for varying sizes and hardness of stone.

- A little jar of Testor's™ model paint (a high-quality enamel that works on nearly every surface) will last for years – just be sure to clean the threads after each use to keep air out of the jar.

- Get the smallest artist's brush you can find, and acetone to clean it. Nail polish remover will not work because it also contains water. Care for your brush and it'll last you 20 years.

- You will want a pad to work on, to keep the stones steady and cushion your hands. An old towel folded in quarters works fine. Be sure to take it outside and shake the stone dust out of it regularly.

- Equipment you must have – and I mean *must* – is eye and lung protection. Glasses will do for your eyes but goggles are better. The kind of white fiber dust mask used by house painters is sufficient and *required*. I'm speaking me to you here: I didn't bother with a mask for years, inhaled a lot of rock & glass dust, and now I have nodules on my lungs. Please don't be that heedless.

But say you don't want to invest that much money right now or get that complicated? There's a much simpler way. Choose porous rocks like sandstone or limestone. Or little discs of wood from the crafts store. Mark the Runes on them with a Sharpie™. The spirit-based ink will seep in and be more or less permanent.

In either case, you will need to select more stones than the set requires, for the simple reason that you *will* mess up. After more than forty years I still mess up, so I can guarantee you will, especially at first and especially if you use real stones. The glass globs are the same texture throughout; real stones can have soft or hard spots that make the line thicker or thinner or go skidding off on a tangent. They also have an annoying habit of twisting out of your fingers.

So...

- Select your stones; unless you're using glass globs, they will come in a variety of shapes, so try, while keeping them all approximately the same size, to match the stone to the symbol, the symbol to the stone.

- Choose querent stones of a contrasting color though about the same size, a longish one for the male stone and a round one for the female. If you decide to include a "group" or "genderless" querent, you will want to choose a stone of still a third color or a radically different shape. Just remember that they have to feel comfortable in your hands, so no jagged edges.

- The first time you make a set you will want to make a few practice stones first from your "slush pile." If they come out well, so much the better, but if you have problems you won't be ruining any you particularly liked.

- Work slowly. It's not required to make the whole set at one go.

- Don't be afraid to discard ones that didn't come out quite the way you envisioned, even if technically they're OK. You'll get better divination results from a set you love.

- Paint over the engraved lines. Try to stay in the lines but if you don't it's not the end of the world: the paint outside the lines will chip off as you use the stones. Depending on how much you use them you'll need to touch up the paint every few years, while the stones will take on a lovely patina from the oils in your hands.

- When they're finished and dry, put them in a nice bag the right size. I make mine but if you don't enjoy sewing, magical-looking small pouches are available in mystical shops and import stores nearly everywhere.

- You may also want to get or make a box to store this book (if you're reading this in paperback) and your Witches Runes set. One with a latch or ties is very helpful when you travel with your set – for instance, when you start doing readings!

If you'd like a set of The Witches' Runes but aren't confident you could make your own, I do still make them for sale. My contact information is at the back of the book.

Unlike many crafters of magical supplies, I make a point of *not* blessing or charging anything I make for sale. That's for you, their owner, to do if you wish. My energies might interfere with your own or be incompatible. And there's an old saying among Witches that the best way to charge a magical tool is to use it!

BIBLIOGRAPHY

Blum, Ralph. *The Book of Runes*. St. Martin's Press, 1979

Crowther, Arnold & Patricia. *Lid Off the Cauldron*. Samuel Weiser, Inc., 1981

Cooper, D. Jason. *Using The Runes*. Aquarian Press, 1987

Farrar, Janet & Stewart. *The Witches' Way* (U.K.) Robert Hale, Ltd., 1981 also released as
A Witch's Bible (U.S.). Magickal Childe, 1984

Hartsfvang, Bjoern-Erik. *Nine Worlds and Three Wells: An Exploration of Norse Cosmology*. Self-Published, 1988

Howard, Michael A. *The Runes & Other Magical Alphabets*. Samuel Weiser, 1978

Pennick, Nigel. *Rune Magic*. Aquarian Press, 1992

Ryall, Rhiannon. *West Country Wicca*. Phoenix Publishing, 1989

Thorsson, Edred. *Futhark: A Handbook of Rune Magic*. Samuel Weiser, 1984

Dennis, Kingsley. *Re-enchanting the World*. https://kingsleydennis.com September 11th, 2017

Atwater, P.M.H. *The Magical Language of the Runes*. Bear & Co., 1986 Updated and re-issued as *Goddess Runes*. Avon, 1996

> <u>Note</u>: The "woman from California" mentioned in the Introduction to Atwater's book is myself; I sold her her first set. Ms. Atwater's method is a radical off-shoot from this one: she has altered the order and changed many of the core meanings of the Runes, and given her version a complex feminist philosophical slant. A fascinating look at how symbols evolve, and a worthwhile system in its own right.

Dana Corby has been a Witch since 1971, during which time she participated in the formation of the Covenant of the Goddess, co-edited the now-classic "Crystal Well," and helped create the genre of Pagan recording by facilitating and performing on Gwydion Pendderwen's pioneering "Songs for the Old Religion."

Her writings have appeared in Pagan journals for over forty years, on "The Rantin' Raven" blog on the Patheos Pagan Agora, and in the anthology "Keepers of the Flame: Interviews with Wiccan Elders," edited by Aradia Lynch and Morgana Davies (Phoenix Press.)

Not only a writer and musician, Dana's also a practical artist. Her shop on

the Facebook Marketplace, called The Witches Runes and More, offers such diverse Pagan tchotchkes as travel shrines, padded wand cases, nature jewelry, spell boxes, and Pagan-themed decorative switchplates for your ritual space.

These days she and her husband live on a wooded island in Puget Sound.

You can contact Dana at danacorby@centurytel.net or find her on Facebook.

Made in the USA
Coppell, TX
19 June 2020

28713546R00028